HOW TO DRAW YOUR OWN GRAPHIC NOVEL

DRAWING ACTION IN YOUR GRAPHIC NOVEL

FRANK LEE

PowerKiDS press™

New York

Published in 2012 by The Rosen Publishing Group, Inc.

29 East 21st Street, New York, NY 10010

Copyright © 2012 Arcturus Publishing Limited

Text and Illustrations: Frank Lee with Jim Hansen and Peter Gray

Editors: Joe Harris and Kate Overy

U.S. Editor: Kara Murray

Design: Andrew Easton

Cover Design: Andrew Easton

Library of Congress Cataloging-in-Publication Data

Lee, Frank, 1980–

Drawing action in your graphic novel / by Frank Lee.

p. cm. —— (How to draw your own graphic novel)

Includes index.

ISBN 978-1-4488-6477-5 (library binding) —— ISBN 978-1-4488-6451-5 (pbk.) ——

ISBN 978-1-4488-6452-2 (6-pack)

1. Action in art--Juvenile literature. 2. Figure drawing—— Technique—— Juvenile literature. 3. Comic books, strips, etc.—— Technique—— Juvenile literature. I. Title.

NC785.L44 2012

741.5'1——dc23

2011027678

Printed in China

SL002068US

CPSIA Compliance Information: Batch #AW2102PK: For Further Information contact Rosen Publishing, New York, New York at 1-800-237-9932

CONTENTS

DRAWING TOOLS

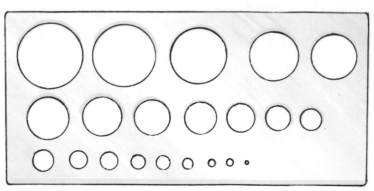

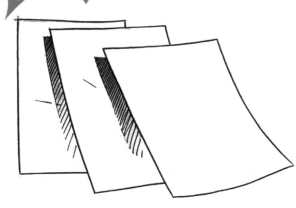

CIRCLE TEMPLATE

This is very useful for drawing small circles.

LAYOUT PAPER

Most professional illustrators use cheaper paper for basic layouts and practice sketches before they get around to the more serious task of producing a masterpiece on more costly paper. It's a good idea to buy some plain paper from a stationery shop for all of your practice sketches. Go for the least expensive kind.

DRAWING PAPER

This is a heavy-duty, high-quality paper, ideal for your final version. You don't have to buy the most expensive brand. Most decent art or craft shops stock their own brand or a student brand and, unless you're thinking of turning professional, these will do fine.

WATERCOLOR PAPER

This paper is made from 100 percent cotton and is much higher quality than wood-based papers. Most art shops stock a large range of weights and sizes. Paper that is 140 pounds (300 g/m) should be fine.

FRENCH CURVES

These are available in a few shapes and sizes and are useful for drawing curves.

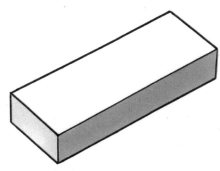

ERASER

There are three main types of eraser: rubber, plastic, and putty. Try all three to see which kind you prefer.

PENCILS

It's best not to cut corners on quality here. Get a good range of graphite (lead) pencils ranging from soft (#1) to hard (#4).

Hard lead lasts longer and leaves less graphite on the paper. Soft lead leaves more lead on the paper and wears down more quickly. Every artist has their personal preference, but #3 pencils are a good medium range to start out with until you find your favorite.

Spend some time drawing with each weight of pencil and get used to their different qualities. Another good product to try is the mechanical pencil. These are available in a range of lead thicknesses, 0.5 mm being a good medium range. These pencils are very good for fine detail work.

PENS

There is a large range of good-quality pens on the market these days and all will do a decent job of inking. It's important to experiment with different pens to determine which you are most comfortable using.

You may find that you end up using a combination of pens to produce your finished artwork. Remember to use a pen that has waterproof ink if you want to color your illustration with a watercolor or ink wash. It's a good idea to use one of these anyway. There's nothing worse than having your nicely inked drawing ruined by an accidental drop of water!

BRUSHES

Some artists like to use a fine brush for inking linework. This takes a bit more practice and patience to master, but the results can be very satisfying. If you want to try your hand at brushwork, you will definitely need to get some good-quality sable brushes.

MARKERS

These are very versatile pens and, with practice, can give pleasing results.

INKS

With the dawn of computers and digital illustration, materials such as inks have become a bit obscure, so you may have to look harder for these. Most good art and craft shops should stock them, though.

DYNAMIC POSES

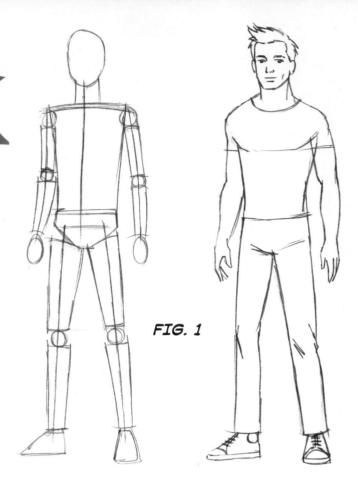

FIG. 1

This book is all about action. You will learn how to make your comic-book panels and covers more interesting by animating your characters. As you develop your figure-drawing skills, you will be able to transform simple stances into explosive action poses!

STANDING READY

Take a look at the two figures on this page. The first character (Fig. 1) is standing in a lifeless, uninteresting pose. However, the second character (Fig. 2) looks ready for action. Look at the construction diagrams that show how the two figures were composed, and you'll see some important differences. Even if your character is just standing still, the use of dynamic figure poses brings him to life. This will make your comic-book pages look more much exciting.

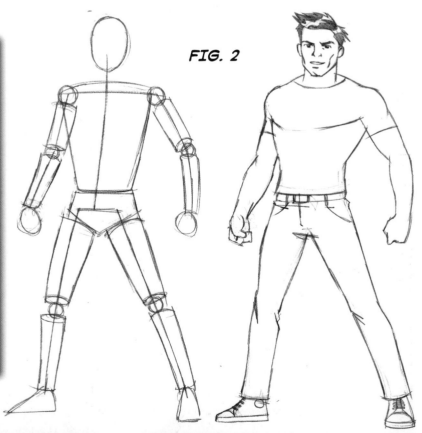

FIG. 2

ACTING THE PART
Imagine that you are a director and your characters are actors. What does their performance tell us? These two characters may be standing still, but their poses tell us immediately that they are confident and powerful.

STRIKE A POSE!
The barbarian (above) has his legs spread wide and holds his arms away from his body. This tells us he is ready for battle. The superheroine (right) has her hands on her hips and one knee bent. This tells us she is sassy and self-assured.

RUNNING: FRONT VIEW

Let's get moving! Here are some running poses viewed from the front. The second version (Fig. 2) is more dynamic. You can really feel the action. It looks like the figure could leap off the page towards you! Try to choose poses that feel high-powered and energetic. These will make your graphic novel feel action packed.

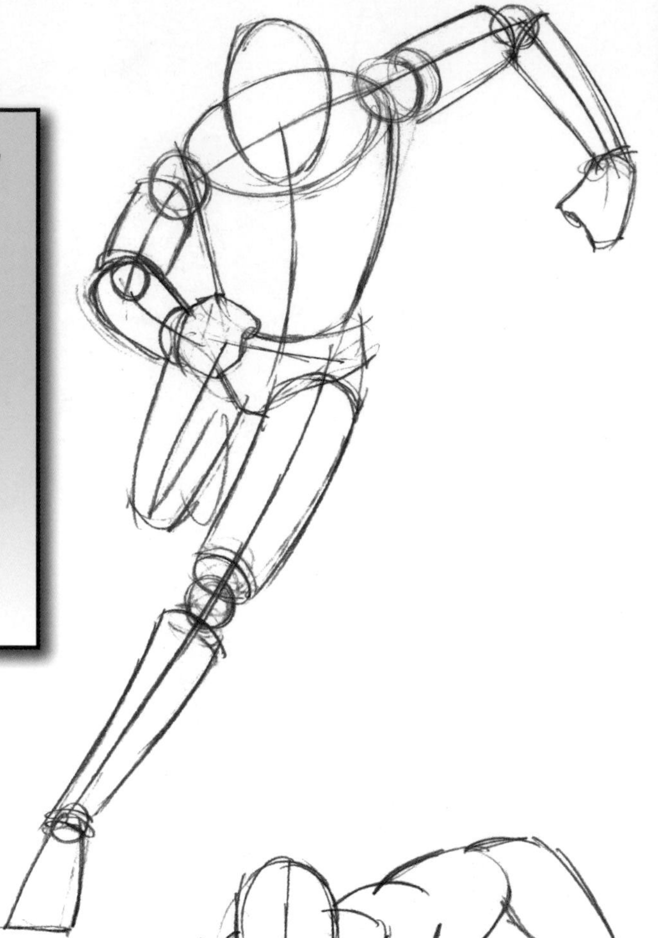

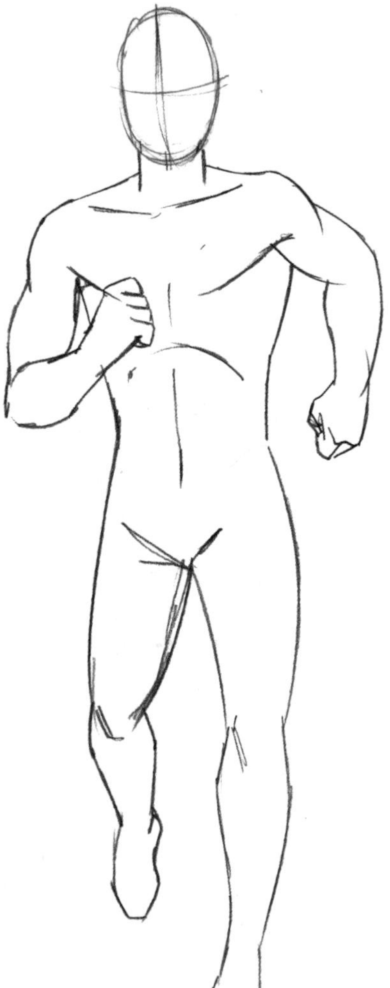

FIG. 1

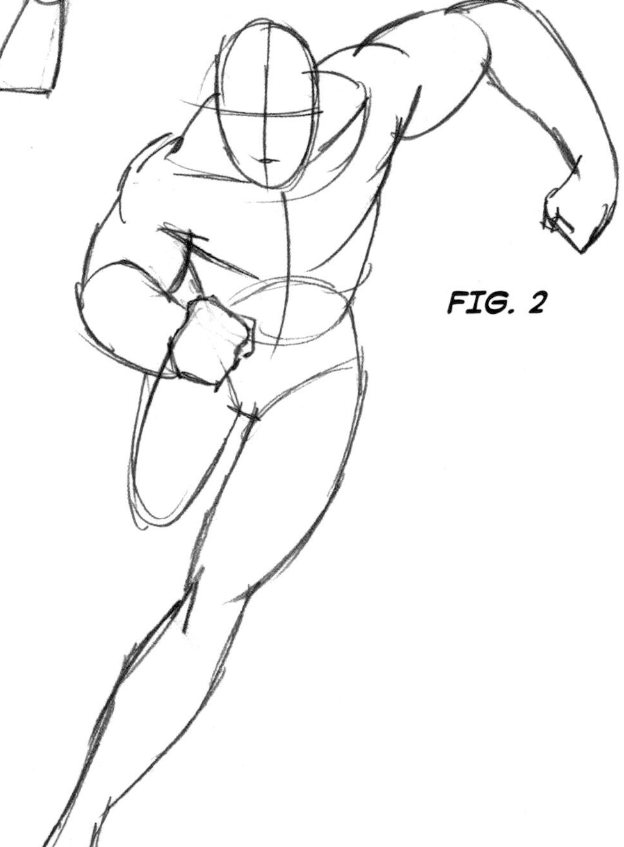

FIG. 2

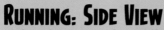

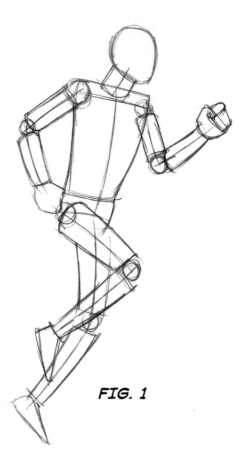

RUNNING: SIDE VIEW

Look at the images of two different side-view running poses below. Which one do you find more interesting? The figure in a casual running pose on the left (Fig. 1)? Or the figure on the right who looks like he's about to take off (Fig. 2)? No contest! Sometimes it helps to start off with a more boring pose then exaggerate the action you're drawing gradually, in stages, until you end up with a really exciting pose.

FIG. 1

FIG. 2

STEP BY STEP: RUN FOR IT!

Here's a step-by-step guide to drawing, inking, and coloring a running character. The main thing about this pose is that it's not balanced. If you tried to stand like this yourself, you would fall over. That imbalance helps give the impression of movement.

STEP 1

Draw the character's head, chest, and pelvis first. You are drawing her body from the side but with it leaning forward so the body parts follow a diagonal line. Now add the limbs.

STEP 2

Draw the outline shape of her flesh and muscle. Notice how there are strong curves in the shape at the backs of the legs to show her strong muscles.

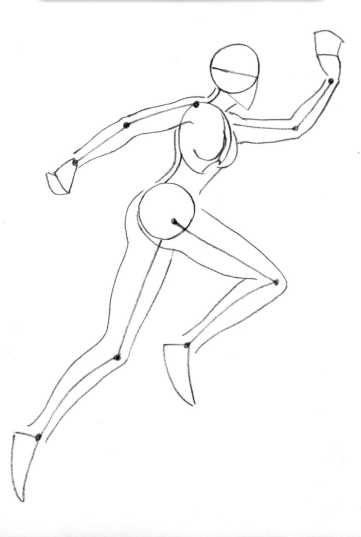

STEP 3

Add some basic lines for her tunic and cloak. Add the main features of the face and some of the curves of the hair. Work on the shape of the feet.

STEP 4

Give the clothing more detail. Notice the square-shaped neck of the tunic. Draw some lines along the bottom of the skirt and cloak to show the folds. Work on the hands and feet. She is wearing sandals, so you'll still be able to see her toes in the final picture.

STEP 5

Once you're happy with your drawing, go over your pencil lines in ink. Now add some shading to the hair to give it more depth.

STEP 6

Leave the ink to dry, then erase all your remaining pencil guidelines.

STEP 7
Now you can add some color to your picture. We've given her auburn hair and a green tunic. Notice how dark the inside of the cloak is where it is in shadow.

FIGHTING POSES

If you plan to show your heroes and villains in conflict, you'll need to learn how to draw combat poses.

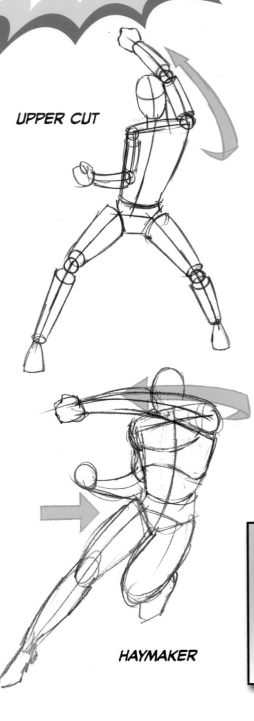

UPPER CUT

HAYMAKER

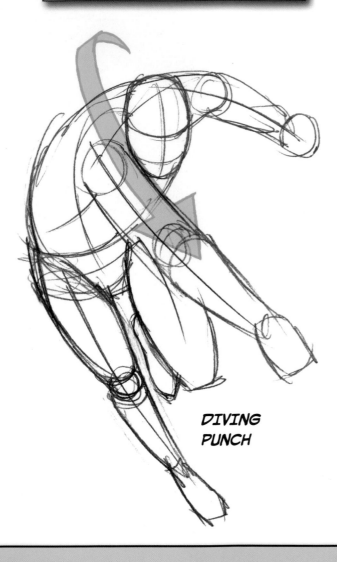

DIVING PUNCH

PUNCHING

To draw a really convincing punch, you have to consider the flow and direction of the action. Look at the three different examples on this page. Arrows have been added to show the flow of action through the body.

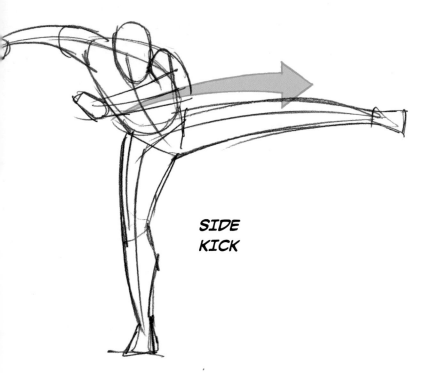

SIDE
KICK

KICKING

Here we have some different types of
dynamic kicking actions. Characters
trained in martial arts are often seen in
kicking poses. These poses show
off their skills in the art of combat. Each
of these figures is delivering a different
type of kick.

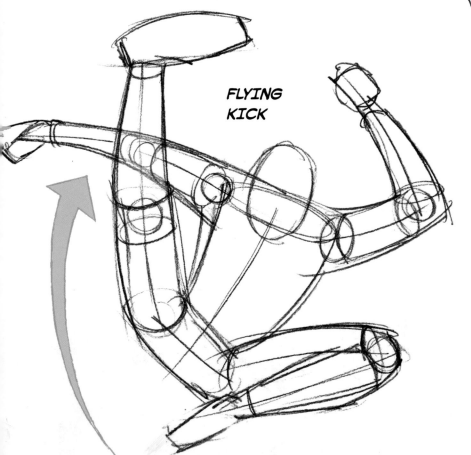

FLYING
KICK

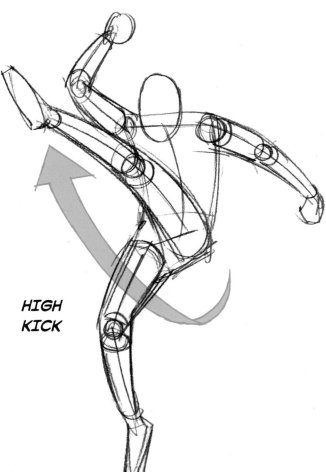

HIGH
KICK

STEP-BY-STEP: FIGHTING HERO

This hero has his right hand pulled back, ready to deliver a wall-smashing punch.

STEP 1
Start by creating the loose, skeletal stick figure.

STEP 2
Start to flesh out the figure using the construction shapes.

STEP 3
Now begin to develop the outer form of the figure, adding basic muscle detail. At this stage you should keep your pencil sketch loose and light.

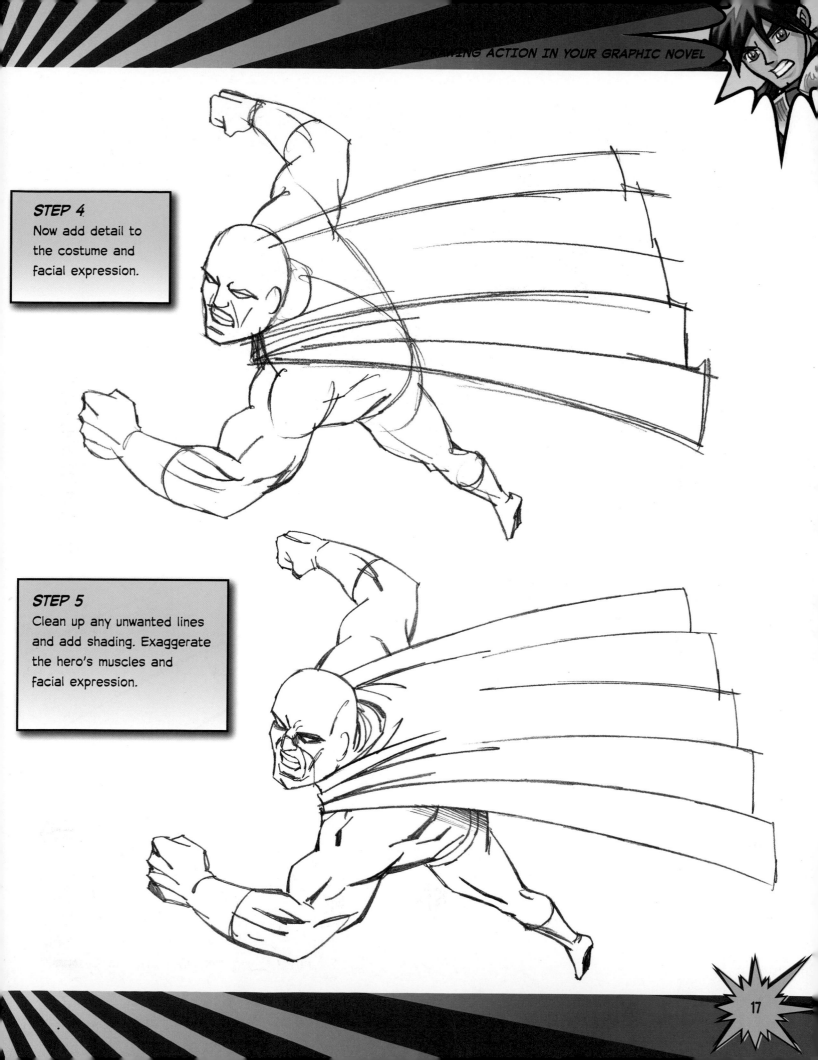

STEP 4
Now add detail to the costume and facial expression.

STEP 5
Clean up any unwanted lines and add shading. Exaggerate the hero's muscles and facial expression.

STEP 6

Find the strongest pencil lines and go over them in ink. Add darker areas to define his muscles and to give his cape more weight.

STEP 7

The hero's cape billows out behind him as he lunges forward. This gives the image a real sense of movement. Individually shade each fold of the cape to make it look three-dimensional.

WEAPONS IN ACTION

Here we have a series of action poses showing combat using a weapon. Think about the direction of the action and then make your character's body follow it. The key is to capture a dramatic movement in a few simple lines. Once you have captured the flow of action, you can refine the figure by adding more detail.

SHOWING SPEED

How can you show that something is happening quickly when your images are static? The answer is speed lines. These are a great way of conveying not just rapid movement, but also intensity and power.

Radial speed lines (such as in the image above) give a feeling of forwards or backwards movement. Speed lines can also be horizontal, angular, or vertical (see below).

HORIZONTAL

AT AN ANGLE (FOLLOW THE LINES OF PERSPECTIVE)

VERTICAL

FLOWING MOVEMENTS

The key to drawing great action is to capture a dramatic movement in a few simple lines. Once you have captured the flow of action, you can refine the figure by adding more detail. At this stage you can make sure the proportions are correct.

Our first character is built around two lines (in red) shaped like an X.

This second character has a simple diagonal line as his starting point.

Capes and hair can play an important role in creating a sense of flowing, directional movement.

STEP BY STEP: FLYING HEROINE

Superhero characters should look like they are in dynamic movement as they fly.

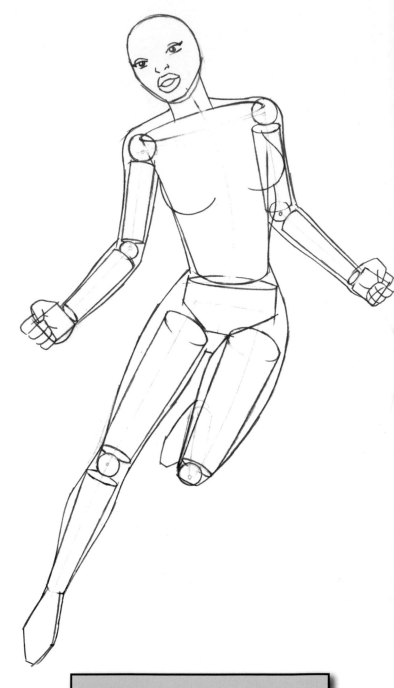

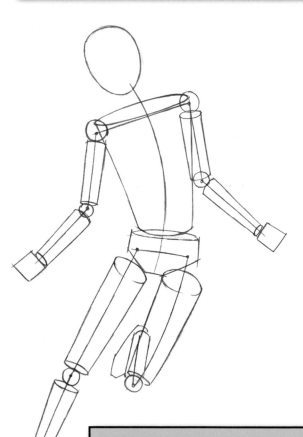

STEP 1
Draw the superheroine's flying pose using a stick figure, then build on it with the basic construction shapes.

STEP 2
Add the facial features and define the figure by smoothing out the construction shapes. When you are happy with how it looks, draw an outline around the shapes.

STEP 3

Once you have defined the shape of the body, remove your rough lines and shapes and start penciling in her costume. We've chosen a classic superhero style—a spandex suit, a cape, and a mask.

STEP 4

Clean up the pencil work and add any final details. Shade in any areas that will be inked in solid black.

STEP 5
Now carefully ink over your pencil work to make your drawing bolder.

STEP 6

Choose a color scheme that complements the character, using a palette that's pleasing to the eye. We have chosen a simple two-color scheme of red and yellow, but there are endless possibilities! Try adapting the colors and suit design to create your own superheroine!

GLOSSARY

construction shapes (kun–STRUK–shun SHAYPS) Shapes such as blocks and balls, which are drawn over a stick figure to make it more three–dimensional.

directional movement (dih–REK–shun–ul MOOV–ment) In a drawing, this is the impression that a figure is moving in a certain direction, such as forward and out of the page toward the reader.

director (dih–REK–ter) The person who decides how a movie or stage play should be performed. For example, the director tells actors how to move and what emotions they should recreate.

flow of action (FLOH UV AK–shun) The movements that flow through a body during an action such as running or jumping.

layouts (LAY–owts) Sketches that show where items, such as figures and words, will be positioned on each page.

lines of perspective (LYNS UV per–SPEK–tiv) The angled lines in a drawing that give an impression of depth or distance.

matchstick figure (MACH–stik FIH–gyur) A simple drawing of a person using sticks and circles.

proportions (pruh–POR–shunz) The sizes of different parts of a figure in comparison to each other. For example the head should be sized according to the figure's height.

speed lines (SPEED LYNZ) Drawn or painted lines (often in the background) that give the impression that an object or person is moving fast.

Further Reading

Besel, Jennifer M. *The Captivating, Creative, Unusual History of Comic Books (Unusual Histories)*. Mankato, MN: Capstone Press, 2010.

Hitch, Bryan. *Bryan Hitch's Ultimate Comics Studio*. New York, NY: Impact, 2010.

Lee, Stan. *Stan Lee's How to Draw Comics*. New York, NY: Watson-Guptill, 2010.

Rosinsky, Natalie M. *Write Your Own Graphic Novel*. Mankato, MN: Compass Point Books, 2008.

Slate, Barbara. *You Can Do a Graphic Novel*. New York, NY: Alpha Books, 2010.

Templeton, Ty; Delaney, John; Boyd, Ron; Foster, Walter. *How to Draw Batman and the DC Comics Super Heroes*. Irvine, CA: Walter Foster Publishing, 2000.

Web Sites

Due to the changing nature of Internet links, Rosen Publishing has developed an online list of Web sites relating to this subject. This website is updated regularly. Please use this link to access the site:

www.powerkidslinks.com/hdgn/action/

INDEX

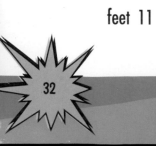